I0756245

FINISHING LINE PRESS
www.finishinglinepress.com

Recipe for a Funeral

poems by

Mary Eichbauer

Finishing Line Press
Georgetown, Kentucky

Recipe for a Funeral

To my family,
with thanks for their loving support
and unfailing inspiration:
Greg, Nate, Sarah, Scarlett, Joelle, and Henry

Copyright © 2026 by Mary Eichbauer
ISBN 979-8-89990-448-6 First Edition
All rights reserved under International and Pan-American Copyright Conventions. No part of this book may be reproduced in any manner whatsoever without written permission from the publisher, except in the case of brief quotations embodied in critical articles and reviews.

ACKNOWLEDGMENTS

I owe friends and family more thanks than I can possibly express here. Every one of the people I care for has made a difference in my life that led me to these poems.

Thank you to my poetry critique group (Johanna Ely, Laurie Hailey, Deborah Bachels Schmidt, and Beth Tarpley) for years of caring friendship and mutual inspiration. Thanks to Wendy Anderson, Helen Bickford, Joyce Hsiao, Linda Hastings, Kathleen Resch, Lois Requist, and Bob Stanley for their enduring friendship. I treasure the memory of magical hours spent in Wendy's art studio, where I learned how to see.

My gratitude for their generosity to Sandra Anfang, the late Jack Foley, Sarah Gartrell, Linda Hastings, and Jan Malin. I am grateful to my dear friend Tom Stanton for allowing me to reproduce a detail from his luminous painting "St. Catherine's Wood," a view of the Carquinez Strait from Benicia.

Publisher: Leah Huete de Maines
Editor: Christen Kincaid
Cover Art: Thomas Eric Stanton—"St. Catherine's Wood" (detail)
Author Photo: Sarah Gartrell
Cover Design: Elizabeth Maines McCleavy

Order online: www.finishinglinepress.com
also available on amazon.com

Author inquiries and mail orders:
Finishing Line Press
PO Box 1626
Georgetown, Kentucky 40324
USA

Contents

Never Happened

...but I would only remember
how I woke to familiar fragrance,
late roses, bruised apples...
—H.D., Helen in Egypt

Tricky memory—
many evenings
when the sun sets too soon,
sparking through windows,
refracted by glassware,
smoldering through bottles
of burgundy wine,

I toil to write a poem,
brain besieged by mementoes.
Threads in a loom
suddenly snap—
dart up like snakes,
then droop into sodden hair.

They say that scent
holds the key to memory,
childhood moments
barely recalled—
ripe fruit, summer tomatoes,
pears rotting on the lawn,
consumed by ravenous wasps

who gulped down the pearly flesh
as we stood by and watched,
senses gorged on the floral perfume
of late summer harvests,
never quite remembering
why or what we were.

Coyote

She drove home from the hospital
at 4:30 in the morning
through a desolate world.

Without the person
she cared for most,
what was left?

On a forsaken highway,
she stopped at a red light,
and then she saw the coyote

standing there, watching her,
looking deep into her eyes.
As they stared, he told her

everything he knew:
about time, how it only moves
in one direction;

about life, how it only comes
to one conclusion;
about her sorrow,

how indifferent he was to it;
how the natural world
turns a blank face

to human tears.
Many years later
she would remember

the moment he loped off
down the empty road,
having shown her everything
she needed to know.

To One I Left Behind

In the dead of night
when the clocks stop
and time falls
into black oblivion
you return
as a furred, sharp-toothed
thing, paws pattering
on the deck
outside my window
making a marimba
of the resonant boards

You trill and hum
a siren song
calling me to slip
through the window
and join
your nighttime
rambles

My cat steals
off the bed
to hide

The dogs snuffle uneasily
in their sleep

A few drops of rain
patter on leaves,
the night wind
rises like a breath,

and the spell is broken.
Time starts again.

This Dry Raisin My Heart

My mother taught me
to keep my heart in a memory box,
set apart like a precious gem,
never to take it out,
never to look at it
except to make sure
it was still there,
still safe.

She kept her heart so long
it shrank to a nub,
rattled around in the bottom drawer
of her wooden jewelry box.

She is gone, long since,
and that small sarcophagus
sits on my dresser,
filled with beads and trinkets,
charms and ornaments,
a golden cameo
with the face of a sphinx.
When I open that box,
a faint tendril of her perfume
still unfurls.

My mother showed me
that hearts are not for sharing,
that treasures must be saved
until everyone who might want them
has passed on. Now, too late,
I search through what she left me,
to find chains jumbled in a snarl,
protecting a withered heart.

And so, my dear,
if I don't reveal my heart to you,
if the only sign of it you see

is the ghostly essence
of a desiccated fruit
enclosed by golden strands,
then you should know
that somewhere,
in a dark and hidden place,
my heart is throbbing still,
and the cadence it beats out
is the rhythm of your name.

Motherless

Little Nancy's father was a burly cop,
who, every Saturday, lurched up
the stone walk to the house
where Nancy lived with her aunts,
two thin women with pinched faces
who never left the house,
never let another child inside.

She hated me, that motherless girl—
glared at me
with her pale, freckled face
in a halo of wispy hair.
Her gingham dresses were a size too large,
sagging on her spare frame.
Do you remember? she would coax,
sidling up to my mother's apron,
reaching for her arms.
Do you remember when you were my mother?

My mother never said yes,
but she never said no,
and it startled me,
made me wonder if it was true,
if there was something crucial I had forgotten.

When Nancy came to the house,
she grabbed my toys, pinched me,
wormed her way between me and my mother,
shoved me away from my mother's knees,
trying to keep all the mothering for herself
and leave me with nothing.

She couldn't know
that the mother she coveted
had already abandoned me once,
that I wasn't entirely sure she was back,
that she wouldn't leave again,

or that she was the same mother
who had left me in the hospital.
Is that when she was Nancy's mother,
while I was somewhere else?

Maybe I had another mother somewhere
who hadn't left me to the doctors,
who didn't scream and hit.
Maybe we were both motherless girls,
looking for some kind of miracle.

Cosmos

As a child, I remember
first seeing these flowers,
pushing up through the weeds
in my mother's unkempt garden—
pink, white, or darker pink,
striated petals, delicate as wings,
surrounding a yellow center
of bright flecks,
each bloom a small explosion.

The long green stems,
with their ferny leaf fingers
smelled earthy, minty,
when I squeezed them
between my little fingers,
or when I crushed
the faded blooms
to release a shower
of sickle-shaped seeds
that dropped through the weeds
to the soil below.

My mother told me their name,
starting with a percussive, hard "c,"
then the vowel,
said with an open mouth,
like the sound a crow makes,
but the rest escaped
into other sounds—
an "m," an "s"—
too sibilant, unpronounceable.
She said it over and over
as I struggled to repeat it,
and the beauty of the flower
faded into an echoing forest of sounds.

Years later, in a garden store,
I saw the familiar flower on a paper packet,
recognized the name I couldn't say,
was too young to read—
cosmos, two syllables,
encompassing the universe.

Charlie

Everyone knew Charlie.
"Left back" over and over again,
he'd been in the sixth grade forever,
older than he should have been.
His voice was gruff, his words
hard to understand.
Even the boys who made fun of him
feared to go too far. He was strong
and he punched hard.

I don't know how or why
he started trailing me that bright Saturday,
down Hickory Street,
into my neighborhood,
or why I was alone, at loose ends,
a little girl on a summer's day
without a friend or a parent.

He spoke to me, and I answered,
remembering to be polite,
in my seven-year-old way,
not revealing the worry
gathering in my chest, tightening
my belly, the sense
that this wasn't right,
that he and I shouldn't be
together, alone.

In front of my house,
I started to feel safe
until I remembered
my parents weren't home.
The house stared blandly,
blind and empty. The garage door
gaped open the width of my body.
From inside, the chill darkness called.

But Charlie was there,
saying something,
asking if it was my house,
his eyes darting to the yawning door
and back to me,
a look I didn't recognize,
a sly look, covetous,
glancing both ways, up and down
the hot, deserted street.

And then for an instant I saw myself
from outside, above,
a little girl in her Saturday clothes,
hesitating on the sidewalk
in front of her empty house,
a morsel for his hunger,
about to be devoured.

I didn't answer him.
Maybe he knew it was my house,
but he didn't stop me,
too irresolute to touch my arm.

I kept walking down the block,
and somewhere I lost him,
I don't remember where,
or how, or if his fear
tugged him away.

He didn't become a monster,
at least not that day.
I walked off alone,
dragging the tattered remnants
of my innocence.

Martens

I am maybe eight or nine years old.

My mother is ready to go out for the evening, shoulders encircled by a chaplet of scrawny dead animals, their little paws hanging limply down, their claws clashing against each other with a soft shhh. They're all sewn together and they can't get away. They still have beady eyes as in life, but those eyes are glass. They're flayed, emptied, their little assholes sewn shut with crosses of black thread. I lift their tails to see. I don't like to look, but I have to keep checking. That's how I know they're real. But, truly, I would prefer it if they weren't.

Like Kali with her string of skulls, my mother with dead martens around her neck.

I have a cat. I love her, I think, but she shreds my hands regularly. She hisses, and her green eyes glower at me. I think she might like to kill me. I try to hold her and pet her, but she runs away. The martens are always available to be mauled. I don't need their consent. But it feels wrong.

I go into the closet to be close to the marten stole. The closet is in a tiny vestibule off the front door of our Tudor-style house. It isn't completely dark in there, because there's a leaded glass window that lets in the light of the season: bright in summer, muted and limpid in winter. The martens are easy to see and examine. I stand there and look at them, and I make up stories.

The marten with his head at the end—he's the chief marten. Beneath his narrow muzzle, instead of his lower jaw, there's a clip that shuts hard. When my mother wears the stole, the clip closes on the tail of the last marten. When I am in the closet, I move the clip that is his jaw to make him talk to me. He tells me things, and I reply. I whisper so we won't be heard. He isn't very nice. When he gets mad, he bites my fingers. I wish I could remember the stories he told. They might have been scary, but I think they must have been wonderful.

I'm not supposed to touch the martens, but I can't keep my hands off. Their fur is silky and rough. I'm fascinated but they horrify me. They talk but they're dead. I dread getting caught in there with them, and I always feel exposed, as if I'm doing something shameful. I don't think about it at the time, but the house must get quiet. It must be obvious that I'm up to no good. And there I am again standing in the closet with the dead martens—their camphor scent, their sewn-shut assholes. Their stories. Their impotent, toothless jaws.

It's a simple piece of apparel to my mother. To me, it's the stuff of nightmares. So why am I in there so often? Because the marten whispers to me about things I'm not supposed to know. Death and pain, and what creatures do to each other's dead bodies. It's ugly in here. It's carnal. I stand among the furs in the bright light of day and look at horrors.

I don't know what happened to the martens, but I suspect that they were not cured well enough. There was always an air of ratty putrefaction about them. Maybe they disintegrated, or maybe she gave them away. I wish they had inflated their flat little bodies and gone back to the snowy tundra of their ancestors.

Who knows what martens talk about when they are in the snow? When they are in closets, they tell secrets that parents don't want you to know. About cruelty. About obsession. About captivity—the fate of all wildness.

Bird Girl

Feather suit, webbed feet of felt,
Koo-Koo the Bird Girl
danced on a table in Freaks,
because the director asked her to,
I guess,
or maybe because she had decided
to embrace it, to seek the gaze
of all those "normals" who came
to see her bird skull,
her chicken-wing arms,
her beak of a nose.

As a child,
I always thought I wanted to see
the Coney Island freak show
until I passed it one day,
on the midway
that smelled of beer, stale popcorn, and pee,
cold wind, no sun,
sand grating under my feet
on the worn-down boardwalk.

The barker beckoned us in,
both arms working like windmills,
straw hat, striped shirt
pulled tight over his gut,
the invariable call of the huckster,
Step right up, step right up and see…

We were invited to look,
to stare at ones born
lacking limbs, or hair,
to gape at misshapen skulls,
at twin girls permanently attached
at the hip.

"Can we go in?" I asked half-heartedly,
because I hadn't seen,
could only imagine,
over the unease in my gut,
what was there to be seen.

My mother huffed by
without a word,
dragging me along.

As we passed the dark maw
of the sideshow,
I already knew that those inside
were human
because I carried scars
on my legs, on my heart,
the dumb cry of *Freak!*
trailing after me
all down the midway,
all through time.

Reenie's Gift

Reenie dragged the oxygen tank
from kitchen to dining room,
Served coffee in her sunlit house,
cups and saucers,
an old-fashioned pattern
with thin gold rims
and tiny flowers.

In the silence,
familiar clatter of bone china cups,
forks against dainty plates,
the steady hiss of Reenie's oxygen,
her labored breath.
We ate Entenmann's coffee cake,
the kind with the sturdy white icing,
so sweet it makes your teeth ache.

Years ago, Reenie and Mom
were young together.
Reenie never married,
made her own way,
bought a house.
Friends sent wedding invitations,
pictures of babies,
toddlers, graduations.

Reenie's voice was urgent.
Not much time now,
each word counted, costly,
none wasted.

"I want you to have these," she said,
pointed at six cordial glasses,
sparkling, filled to the brim with sun,
sapphire blue, daffodil yellow,
emerald, blushing rose,

and a deep, heartbreaking purple,
like the cut glass base
of my grandmother's Victorian lamp.

Reenie died, and soon,
Mom wanted to give the glasses
to a neighborhood rummage sale,
but I took them home,
hoarded them as long as I could,
remembering Reenie's final days,
and then I passed them on
to someone who would
see the sun in them.

Talisman

In our high school class
we were the only ones
afraid to get our ears pierced.
Was it fear,
or our everlasting desire
to be different?

Summer camp, morning "inspection" by the nuns,
to make sure we'd washed,
holding out our hands for Sister,
                    top and palm,
her look of horror at our nacreous green nail polish
speckled with little black dots
we'd inked on with the Koh-i-Noor artist's pen
your father gave you,
and the whole cabin had to stand for inspection again
after we removed the polish.

Years later, you visited me.
We were both in grad school,
                    you were learning conducting—
Un Ballo in Maschera spinning in your CD Walkman—
as usual, we got into trouble,
as always, every man we met swiveled on his axis
like a magnet
and pointed towards you.

At the end of the visit,
I gave you a dress I loved—
                    dusty rose cotton with shell buttons—
that had always looked terrible on me,
and you gave me one of your clip-on rhinestone earrings,
the kind you see in a 50s noir—
                    three strands of diamonds hanging down—
and told me to wear it on one ear
and you would wear the other earring

on your other ear,
because it wasn't cool then
to wear two earrings at once.

I often wondered since
if you regretted giving me that talisman—
the earring that made me your mirror image,
                    your counterpart—
because now it is cool again
to wear two earrings at once, and—
                    now that we don't speak to each other anymore—
you only have one earring.

An Artist Lies Dying

You open your eyes
and the world comes again.
White glare through paper shades,
golden mellow sun slipping under.

It dazzles you, this light,
dissolving, in your watery eyes,
the flowering colors,
as if the tip of a sable-hair brush
kissed wet paper,
sending veins of color sprouting from the center
into flowers or fireworks, starbursts of light.
Outside, irises—yellow or purple,
sky blue or white—
bulbs you chose from a catalog,
watched as they were planted,
waited as they sprouted long arms of green,
flowered in astonishing profusion.

Tongues of flame—
those must be birds,
the robin, a pair of orioles,
the darting hummingbird,
you know them all.
You hear the jay's harsh cry,
remember putting peanuts out,
seeing the jays, the thrashers, the crows
choose them, carry them off,
as the cats watched hungrily from inside,
ready to spring,
digging their claws into your lap.

Warm light.
Under the blankets,
your body slow and cold,
a sluggish burden.
Sleep takes you,

and the dreams begin,
offering a glimpse
into that other world,
just like this one.
Sleeping, waking,
the sun so bright,
birds and flowers,
blue cats-eyes.

Your children, far away,
their distant faces hazy
in late afternoon,
all but one, the youngest,
the one who died so long ago.
Sometimes you see her
standing by your bed,
leaning a little forward,
poised as if to speak, nodding,
smiling, with that quirk you remember
at the corner of her mouth,
that dimple, those hazel eyes.

She danced away, that one,
cost you more heartache than the others,
yet here she is by your bedside,
holding out her hand.

Stone

I heard a story
about a woman
brought to a temple
by her desperate parents

With a stone
the size of her fist
she hammered the slate floor
over and over
now and then she struck a blow
against her forehead
or her chest

When someone
tried to take the stone
she clutched it
and wailed
so they let her
beat out the brutal rhythm
on the floor
on herself

That night
a female postulant
at the temple
lay in bed
next door
hearing the muffled thud
of stone against stone
the absent beat
of stone against flesh
ticking off the seconds
in that rhythm of dumb blows
until it merged
with her own pulse

The student thought
about her family
far away
their love
their lack of love
that drove her away
and brought her back
over and over

And she dreamed
that a woman
lay in utter darkness
hearing the cadence
beaten out
by a woman holding
her heart in her hand
pounding it
over and over again
against unyielding stone

Aunt Minnie's Apple Cake

From *The New Moosewood Cookbook*
Inauguration Day, 20 January 2025

Today, a strange hush
has fallen over town.
Maybe people are enjoying
the late winter sunlight—
or are they reflecting
on the changes coming to our lives?

The oligarchs prevailed today,
the ones who only care about power,
who esteem themselves above the earth,
above us all.

Today, not knowing what else to do,
I will light the oven, and I will bake a cake
from a recipe I've often used,
for friends, for birthdays,
or just for pleasure, when I wanted
to scent the house with apples,
cinnamon, and cardamom—
a fragrance so delicious and sweet
you can taste it on the air.

I'll use flour and brown sugar,
oil from sunflowers,
apples that might have been picked
by people who soon will be deported.
My backyard chickens will give their eggs,
to make the cake tender
and meltingly rich on the tongue.

Today, I will make an apple cake for the ones I love,
for family and friends,
but I long to make a cake for the whole world,
the world that aches today

with disappointment and dread.
I wish I could bake a cake so superb,
so colossal, that,
in other places, far away from me,
people would turn their faces into the wind,
wondering, *What is that delicious fragrance?*
Where is it coming from?
and then, one after another,
they would decide
that today is the perfect day to bake a cake.

They would gather their ingredients,
light their ovens, and fill their neighborhoods
with baking smells, the kinds of smells
that make people think of their stomachs
instead of money, or war,
aromas that bring to mind
sweet and delicious flavors
instead of power,
flavors that make people want to sit down
with others and talk, to drink their favorite tea—
the one that goes so well with sweets—
to share a confection heavy with
apples or honey, with nuts,
and sugar, and oil or butter,
and remember that the world
doesn't have to be the way it is now.

We don't have to fight,
we don't have to bow down to profit,
or hate,
because nothing can resist
the almighty scent of apples and cardamom,
the irresistible urge to feed each other.

Mother's Day

In their coop
the chickens wail
like lost souls
to celebrate the arrival
of another sterile egg

The refrigerator fills
with eggs,
large and small,
green, brown, ecru,
more than we can eat
and so we offer them
to neighbors and friends

Do the hens think they're fertile,
like menopausal mothers
who long in dreams
for their unborn children,
warm, silky armfuls
of living, milky flesh?

Infertile now, old women,
like hens without a rooster,
once passed on
the coiled-up DNA
of generations

On Mother's Day,
the young mother
wants to be alone.
Of course she does,
tired of life
as a metonym—
teat, hands, voice, lap—
wanting, for a moment,
to be human,
to find herself again

So she sends her children
to grandma's house
where they dash
through dappled sunlight
to the chicken coop,
open the door
to the laying box,
the secret chamber
full of straw and feathers,
to find what wonders
nestle there—
warm eggs
to feed the generations.

Sheep Clouds

Cielo pecorino, piove stasera o domani mattino.
(Sheep sky, rain tonight or tomorrow morning.)
—Sicilian proverb

Sheep clouds troop from horizon to horizon,
cotton puffs in their bright blue pasture,
migrating slowly through the skies,
portending rain.

Sicilian women know
that heavy weather threatens,
when the clouds look
as innocent as little lambs.

Wolves in sheep's clothing
masquerade as powder puffs,
hauling behind them
dark clouds, rain, and all the rest—
lightning, floods, roiling rivers.

Late at night,
after the flock passes,
the wind howls in,
slavering at their heels.

Palermo

In Palermo it's 83 degrees,
light wind from the southwest.
Later, they foresee severe weather—
thunderstorms, swollen clouds,
plump raindrops dashing against cobblestones
as people take shelter under awnings,
hop from one foot to the other
while they hold dripping umbrellas
and gossip with the shopkeepers.

In Palermo,
as in all the other places I will never go,
late afternoon turns cool and sultry.
Fitful breaths of wind promise
a change in the weather.

It's the hour of the *riposo*,
when the shopkeepers close their doors,
cover their wares,
and return to their beds—
sheets slightly damp,
covers still rumpled—
for an hour's rest.

Later, red wine
in the café down the street
with a few friends,
quick trip to the vegetable market
for ripe tomatoes that fill your hands
with their warm flesh,
bouquets of broad-leaved basil
that perfume the air.
The fragrance follows you
down the street in a cloud.

What would it be like
to live in a place you had never seen?

The mysterious city you've always heard about
where there are still people
who share your ancestry,
who never waste a thought on you
as they run home laughing from the market
through the rain,
arrange the sprigs of basil in an ordinary jam jar,
set the tomatoes on the windowsill
for later.

Extras

for Jim

Greenwich Village, 1969,
we wandered into
that smudged barroom,
a time capsule of New York bars:
the floor a web of white hexagonal tiles,
the bar a bulwark of mahogany.
Dust motes danced in slanted light
from the open door,
piercing the cool, dim room
on that sizzling New York day,
infusing the dense air with a gauzy haze.

We sat at a table in bent-wood chairs,
while a gaggle of old men hunched at the bar,
their voices loose and low:
old friends enjoying the day,
the whiskey buzz, the hum of conversation.

Joe, the barkeep, lined our martinis up,
icy, transparent,
condensation dripping down the stems,
pooling on scratched wood.

"Hey, Joe," one regular called out,
"Sing 'Old Black Magic.'"
"Yeah, Joe, sing it," chimed in another,
and, eyes widening, looking at each other,
we disappeared
and rematerialized
in a Hollywood movie,
our jeans and summer shirts
morphing into evening wear:
a sequined gown for me;
for you, black tie and tails.

Holding our frozen martinis,
we were extras, watching the scene unfold.
It had nothing to do with us,

but the magic sucked us in,
the hazy air,
the dust motes sparkling like stardust

as Joe quit wiping the bar,
gave us all a big grin,
and, in a low, sultry voice,
tempered by smoke and whiskey,
he sang it.

Recipe for a Funeral

Get a cocktail shaker,
the old-fashioned, shiny metal kind
that reflects your face, distorted
like in a funhouse mirror.

Fill it with ice
and then with all the memories
you can find
of happy times,
of stories that you told,
and I told
(it's okay if you forget—
just make some up),
until you fill all the spaces
between the chunks of ice
with that sweet elixir.

Then blow into it
the breath of life—
pretend it's my soul
and your soul,
together again—
and shake it hard,
hard as you can,
until your fingers tingle
and the metal freezes so hard
your reflection seems covered
in frost and tears.

Then go somewhere we loved—
Paris, maybe?—
or even the end
of the road,
where it hits the strait,
where the palm trees stand,
the place where you can see
two bridges,

where ships go steaming back and forth
from Japan to Sacramento,
where some days the water is blue,
some green,
some days metallic with supple swells.

Then toss me into the wind
and say goodbye.

Later, when the others come,
have plenty of ice
and gin and olives.
(Have vodka for my friends
who don't like gin.)

I wish I could join you,
sit there and drink and chat
in the warm late afternoon,
but I will already be on my way
out to sea,
on my way towards the place
where—
some believe—
we'll all be given
a second chance.

Born in New York City, poet and prose writer **Mary Eichbauer** makes her home in Benicia, California. She was in the first class of women admitted to the California Institute of Technology and holds a BS in Literature. She earned an MA and PhD in Comparative Literature from UCLA, and taught humanities, literature, and writing at UCLA, Long Beach State, and Pitzer College. Her first book of poetry, *After the Opera* (Random Lane Press, 2020), was partly inspired by her extended stays in France and her love of French language and culture. *Love's Meditation* (Random Lane Press, 2023), a collaborative poetry anthology with Johanna Ely, Laurie Hailey, and Deborah Bachels Schmidt, arose out of a long friendship formed during years of meeting as a poetry critique group.

Her poetry has appeared in *Tule Review, The Gathering,* the *Benicia Herald*, and many Benicia First Tuesday Poetry Group anthologies, while her prose writing has appeared in the *Journal of Lesbian Studies* and *Paragraph.* A book of literary criticism, *Poetry's Self-Portrait: The Visual Arts as Mirror and Muse in René Char and John Ashbery,* was published by Peter Lang in 1992.

Mary currently serves on the board of the Ina Coolbrith Circle, the oldest poetry organization in California, and as Editor-in-Chief of Benicia Literary Arts.

www.ingramcontent.com/pod-product-compliance
Lightning Source LLC
LaVergne TN
LVHW090540110826
845146LV00003B/1190

* 9 7 9 8 8 9 9 9 0 4 4 8 6 *